INTIMIDATING

ELEPHANTS

areth Stevens
BLISHING

BY MARY MOLLY SHEA

Please visit our website, www.garethstevens.com. For a free color catalog of all our high-quality books, call toll free 1-800-542-2595 or fax 1-877-542-2596.

Cataloging-in-Publication Data

Names: Shea, Mary Molly.
Title: Intimidating elephants / Mary Molly Shea.
Description: New York : Gareth Stevens Publishing, 2017. | Series: Cutest animals...that could kill you! | Includes index.
Identifiers: ISBN 9781482449181 (pbk.) | ISBN 9781482449129 (library bound) | ISBN 9781482449006 (6 pack)
Subjects: LCSH: Elephants–Juvenile literature.
Classification: LCC QL737.P98 S524 2017| DDC 599.6'1–dc23

First Edition

Published in 2017 by
Gareth Stevens Publishing
111 East 14th Street, Suite 349
New York, NY 10003

Copyright © 2017 Gareth Stevens Publishing

Designer: Sarah Liddell
Editor: Therese Shea

Photo credits: Cover, p. 1 Gerrit_de_Vries/Shutterstock.com; wood texture used throughout Imageman/Shutterstock.com; slash texture used throughout d1sk/Shutterstock.com; p. 5 Zhukova Valentyna/Shutterstock.com; p. 6 Anan Kaewkhammul/Shutterstock.com; p. 7 (African forest elephant) Roger de la Harpe/Gallo Images/Getty Images; p. 7 (African savanna elephant) Anup Shah/The Image Bank/Getty Images; p. 9 ISHARA S. KODIKARA/Stringer/AFP/Getty Images; p. 11 Nigel Pavitt/John Warburton-Lee Photography Ltd./AWL Images/Getty Images; p. 13 DIPTENDU DUTTA/Stringer/AFP/Getty Images; p. 15 Gillian Holliday/Shutterstock.com; p. 17 Villiers Steyn/Shutterstock.com; p. 19 MARTIN BUREAU/Staff/AFP/Getty Images; p. 21 Donovan van Staden/Shutterstock.com.

Printed in the United States of America

CPSIA compliance information: Batch #CS16GS: For further information contact Gareth Stevens, New York, New York at 1-800-542-2595.

CONTENTS

Words in the glossary appear in **bold** type the first time they are used in the text.

SO CUTE...
AND DEADLY!

Have you ever seen a mother and baby elephant **cuddle**? They use their **trunks** to gently touch each other. It's like a hug! When you witness this, it's hard to imagine that the usually peaceful **mammals** called elephants can also be deadly.

Elephants are the largest animals on land. They don't use their size to hunt, though. They're herbivores, or plant eaters. You might wonder what makes them so dangerous. You need to know a bit about the elephant's life to understand.

THE DANGEROUS DETAILS

Elephants are smart. They use their trunk to throw rocks at electric fences to break them so they can pass through!

ENORMOUS ELEPHANTS

One reason elephants are so dangerous is their size. These usually gentle giants are very, very large compared to humans.

There are three species, or kinds, of elephants: the African savanna elephant, the African forest elephant, and the Asian elephant. The largest is the African savanna elephant. It can be as tall as 13 feet (4 m) at the shoulder and weigh up to 16,500 pounds (7,484 kg). Even the smallest elephants are more than 6 feet (1.8 m) tall.

ASIAN ELEPHANT

AFRICAN ELEPHANTS HAVE LARGER EARS THAN ASIAN ELEPHANTS. THE EARS HELP THE ELEPHANT GET RID OF EXTRA BODY HEAT.

AFRICAN SAVANNA ELEPHANT

AFRICAN FOREST ELEPHANT

A HUGE HERD

Elephants live in family groups called herds. The herds are made up of females that all belong to the same large family. Female elephants, or cows, stay with their herd their whole life unless the herd grows too large. Then, the herd splits into two groups, so each can find enough food and water for all.

Male elephants, called bulls, live with the herd until they're between 12 and 15 years old. Then, they leave to wander alone or join up with other herds for a time.

THE DANGEROUS DETAILS

An elephant may walk as far as 50 miles (80 km) in a day looking for food.

PLAY-FIGHTING

As bull elephants get older, they begin to look to other males to learn how to act. They play-fight from a young age. This gets them ready to **defend** themselves and their herd when they're older. It also gets them ready to fight other bulls when they're looking for a **mate**.

It's not just young bulls fighting with each other. Older bull elephants have been observed on their knees in order to play-fight with smaller, younger bulls!

BABY ELEPHANTS SOMETIMES PULL EACH OTHER'S TAIL WHEN THEY PLAY-FIGHT!

11

ELEPHANTS GONE WILD!

As bull elephants get older, they enter a state called musth (MUHST) at times. Bulls in musth can be very **aggressive**. Female elephants may let them join a herd for a time to mate. Some bulls get so wild that they may get kicked out of the herd again.

Sometimes bulls in musth get really out of control. Although it doesn't happen often, they've been known to attack people and destroy whole villages! People in an elephant's way can be easily **trampled**.

THE DANGEROUS DETAILS
Musth may last a few days or several months.

12

ELEPHANTS CAN RUN AS FAST AS 25 MILES (40 KM) PER HOUR. THEY'RE HARD TO STOP WHEN THEY'RE OUT OF CONTROL.

TERRIFIC TRUNKS

An elephant's trunk is an amazing body part. It's used to breathe, eat, drink, **communicate**, and handle things. The end of each trunk has one or two **flaps** that are somewhat like fingers. They help an elephant pick up small things.

Elephants also use their trunk for more destructive activities. They may push over a tree in order to eat its leaves more easily. They can tear off tree branches to throw them at enemies. They might even pick up and throw their enemies!

THE DANGEROUS DETAILS
An elephant's trunk contains about 100,000 **muscles**!

TOUGH TUSKS

So what do elephants use to fight if they don't use their trunk? Elephants with tusks have two dangerous **weapons** at all times.

Tusks are large teeth called incisors. They grow throughout an elephant's life. Elephants use them for digging, lifting objects, and stripping bark from trees to eat. They may also use them to **stab** when they're fighting with each other or other animals!

The hard matter that makes up an elephant's tusk is called ivory. Unfortunately for elephants, ivory is valued by their greatest enemy—people.

ELEPHANTS USE THEIR TUSKS SO MUCH THEY MAY WEAR DOWN OR EVEN BREAK. ELEPHANT TUSKS ARE RARELY THE SAME LENGTH!

THE DANGEROUS DETAILS

Almost all African bull elephants and most cows have tusks. Only some Asian bull elephants have them, while almost no Asian cows have them.

17

THE ELEPHANT'S ENEMIES

Elephants are so large that they don't have much to fear from other animals. Lions and tigers may attack an elephant if it's hurt or alone, but elephants live in herds to guard each other from attacks.

Elephants' greatest enemies are people. People hunt and kill elephants for their ivory tusks. Farmers sometimes kill elephants to keep them from eating their crops. An adult elephant may eat more than 500 pounds (227 kg) of plants a day. So a herd can eat a whole farm!

THE DANGEROUS DETAILS

As many as 100,000 elephants were poached, or illegally killed, between 2010 and 2012.

PEOPLE ARE COMING UP WITH WAYS TO KEEP ELEPHANTS OFF FARMLAND WITHOUT HURTING THEM. THIS FARM USES BEES LIVING IN THESE BEEHIVES!

SAVE THE ELEPHANT!

People also push elephants off their land in order to build houses and businesses. Elephants have less land to **roam** and may hurt people they come in contact with. In fact, elephants kill about 100 people in India each year.

Over the last 100 years, African elephant populations have dropped from several million to as few as 470,000. Asian elephant numbers have dropped from about 100,000 to about 50,000. Now, who do you think is more dangerous, people or elephants?

ELEPHANTS' IMPORTANCE

ELEPHANTS IN THE WILD CAN LIVE TO BE ABOUT 60 YEARS OLD IF LEFT ALONE BY HUMANS.

THEY SPREAD SEEDS IN THEIR WASTE, WHICH HELPS NEW PLANTS GROW.

ELEPHANTS' ESSENTIAL ROLES

THEY EAT PLANTS, WHICH CREATES FOREST CLEARINGS AND STOPS WILDFIRES.

THEY DIG IN THE GROUND, WHICH CREATES WATER HOLES FOR OTHER ANIMALS.

21

GLOSSARY

aggressive: showing a readiness to attack

communicate: to share ideas and feelings through sounds and motions

cuddle: to hold something close for comfort or affection

defend: to drive danger or attack away from

flap: a flat piece that's attached to something on one side and can be moved

mammal: a warm-blooded animal that has a backbone and hair, breathes air, and feeds milk to its young

mate: to come together to make babies. Also, one of two animals that come together to make babies.

muscle: one of the parts of the body that allow movement

roam: to wander

stab: to forcefully push a sharp object into something

trample: to injure by stepping heavily on something or someone

trunk: the long, muscular nose of an elephant

weapon: something used to cause someone or something injury or death

FOR MORE INFORMATION

BOOKS

Downer, Ann. *Elephant Talk: The Surprising Science of Elephant Communication.* Minneapolis, MN: Twenty-First Century Books, 2011.

Hanson, Anders. *Elephant.* North Mankato, MN: ABDO, 2014.

Perkins, Wendy. *Elephant.* Mankato, MN: Amicus, 2016.

WEBSITES

Elephant
www.worldwildlife.org/species/elephant
Find out more about the largest land animals and why they're important.

Gentle Giants
www.pbs.org/edens/anamalai/gentle.html
Read more about elephants and how they care for their young here.

INDEX